# HOW TO FIND & CREATE AN ORIGINAL ART MASTERPIECE

## An Art Register for Artists, Curators and the General Public.

By

Anthony David Padgett

Published by
ADP Publishing


First Published 2018
Copyright Anthony Padgett 2018
2nd edition published 2019
3rd edition published 2020

Dedication

To
THE UNDERVALUED

# TABLE OF CONTENTS

# PREFACE

This book is the result of looking into systems of classifying and categorizing the formal qualities of art. It is a phenomenological analysis of the form of what we can see, rather than any ideas and content intended to be conveyed in what we see. I found that such an analysis was missing from art classification systems that were based on art-historical movements and terms. So I turned this idea of a categorization system into a reality as part of an artist residency at the Museum of Lancashire in 2016. I hope that you adopt and adapt the system and have as fruitful an experience of art as I have over the past few years.

Anthony David Padgett

# INTRODUCTION

Ever felt lost for words in front of a work of art. This book
will help you speak with knowledge and real
understanding.

This book is not about following other people's mis-
understanding of art, but about developing and following
your own understanding.

After studying an MA in Theory of Contemporary
Art and Performance Practice I was surprised that there is
no unified body of art theory. There are disjointed
assertions from a number of artists and critics but no
objective criteria. What is supposed to be art theory is
really just a history of art, describing what happened,
rather than analyzing what makes something an artwork.

Analysis often is based on an agenda such as
socialism or feminism. These gain credence in academic
circles but the art market continues on the basis of the
views, tastes and whims of a few influential buyers.

There are conmen and fraudsters in every business.
So given this then the buyer or artist is very prone to
buying or producing non-art in the mistaken belief that it is
art. And to hide behind the lack of standards and critical
analysis in art contemporary art dealers have defined that it
is impossible to define art. In doing this they have failed to
realize their own self-contradiction.

In this book the system will help you pick through
what is actually original in art. It is the beginnings of
categories for an algorithm and perhaps we will eventually
have artificial intelligence helping show us what is original
art.

By using the system you will be able to identify what kind of work has not been produced and so be able to produce your own masterpiece.

As an art historian and theoretician I investigated how artwork is listed in electronic museum management systems and how art gallery collections. I found the taxonomy (terms used) by the Getty's Art and Architecture Thesaurus (AAT) and their Categories for the Description of Works of Art (CDWA) (which are presented as an industry standard in museum and gallery collection management systems) involve thousands of terms that are so specific that they are completely unwieldy. These taxonomies are useful for cataloguing what is already accepted as art. But not for analyzing and challenging whether those works are actually art.

The AAT and CDWA are so complex that many museums and collection management systems do not use them. However, it is a significant development on an earlier 1940s Art Thesaurus by Albert E. Wier which focussed on art personalities and so does not help describe artworks.

Even simpler dictionary definitions such as in the concise "Tate Guide to Modern Art Terms" by Simon Wilson and Jessica Lack present art terms, art movements and techniques that are, again, very specific. Their terms e.g. Cubism and Bricolage, are composed of a number of different features.

Like the AAT these taxonomies make it hard to analyse and cross reference works because their features are not broken down into constituent parts. The advantage of having a list of the constituent parts of a style of art then you can describe an art movement, such as Cubism and Futurism and clearly see what they have in common.

And by making a thorough study of the works you can see what the movements did or didn't do and, if you like, you can then do the work they didn't do – and so make an original work. The quality of the work might not be the greatest – but it will be original.

This assumes that originality is a key feature of true art. However, the system should also explain why the opposite situation. Where we see kitsch, figurative artwork that merely repeats old styles and is usually representational. Yet people like it and call it art. The system should account for how a work can be not formally originally yet can be of a high quality and that people might see it as art. Yet, because one of the features some people (myself included) usually associates with art is originality we would not call it good art.

And the same analysis should be enabled for many contemporary pieces. They may look highly original, but if you look into the history of art very similar works have been done – e.g. Damien Hirst's "The Physical Impossibility of Death in the Mind of Someone Living" 1991 Shark in a glass tank has similarities to Jeff Koon's earlier "One Ball Total Equilibrium Tank" 1985 basketball in a glass tank. Or Tracey Emin's "My Bed" 1998 installation of an unmade bed has similarities to Louise Bourgoise's earlier installation of a made bed in "Red Room Parents" 1994.

These similarities undermine some of the claims to uniqueness and originality of Hirst's and Emin's work – whatever the people selling the work want to claim.

So I hung 500 copies of artworks from 2 copies of "The Art Book" Phaidon in my studio space and systematically categorised them. Not according to art movements, but according to what I saw, phenomenologically, i.e. how things appear. To be of value this system needed to be turned into a usable project. So I created a table of categories and values.

The resulting system of categorisation is a work of art in itself but the next step was to apply the system in creating original works (I currently have made and am making a number of these) and in analysing museum and gallery collections for the better understanding of art in museums.

My partner and I then made a trial, using the system in the art galleries (the Kunstmuseum and the Museum fur Gegenwartskunst) of Basel, Switzerland, looking at both modern and contemporary artworks.

And using the system a statistical analysis of the main works on display in a gallery can be made with the artwork with the most recurring features be identified. And the system can help museum and gallery curators to see what is missing from its collection.

The system looks at stylistic form only. Any thematic content, e.g. love, war, flowers, castles, can be analysed separately. The system doesn't cover this because whilst thematic content is more easily accessible it is also infinitely variable. Often what is considered new art is just the same stylistic form e.g. photo realism with a new thematic subject matter e.g. a previously unrepresented social group. This is an easy innovation and is about the content rather than the form.

I have simplified many elements so that people can have the tools for understanding art and engaging with collections. This can bring increased pleasure and reduce feelings of alienation and intimidation.

The system is a structure whereby analytical tools can be used to help show work styles and themes. It can empower people who feel that their voice is un-heard or who are under-represented.

It is a model for finding the different medium and themes absent from the collection and explores ideas of what is the limit of art. E.g. 2 paintings that are of squares. XXXX Malevich and "Courier II" by Robert Ryman 1985. Whichever came first is the original one. It doesn't matter what the logic is behind the second one. Those reasons might fit in the conceptual category, which is only one feature, and the artist of the original square most likely had their own conceptual reasons for creating the work.

When we can see the list of qualities (see CASE STUDIES) in common then we doubt the originality and art status of the later work - seeing it as derivative at best or just a good example of the style.

Another e.g. Claus Oldenburgh large sculptures of household objects e.g. "Lipstick (Ascending) on Caterpillar Tracks" 1969. These are like renaissance still life paintings or sculptures. The only difference is that they are larger and of modern items. But in essence they are representational artworks and not a great innovation.

As mentioned, this book is a conceptual artwork to be used and applied in looking at other artworks.

Its originality lies in its application of criteria that I seek to be objective with. These are criteria that it appears to be fashionable for the majority of artists, curators and critics to deny are possible to apply in art. They seem to claim that art is subjective. And hide behind this claim when making selection of artwork. Often selecting unoriginal and derivative art mistaking it for the opposite.

Part of the reason why people believe art is purely subjective may be that they feel overwhelmed by the task of seeking objectivity. Yet I believe that the development of artificial intelligence and algorithms will change this.

My system accepts subjectivity by giving each entry a quality rating and allowing that people can still have personal preference for one work over another) but puts subjectivity within objective parameters. The system allows good and bad art to be determined more easily and original art to be identified. When a person looked at a work in the 19th century they used ideas of form and composition and were only partially subjective in their appraisal.

There are currently no objective criterion in modern and contemporary art. I believe that much of it is just fashionable and will have no lasting value. And like much Victorian art is now deemed to be worth little financial value or interest the same will be said of much contemporary and modern art – unless it can show its objective credentials.

# 1 HOW TO USE THE SYSTEM

Using the system couldn't be easier. You are free to scan and copy the pages or produce your own system. The main thing is to start using the system and don't get caught up in definitions.

Take your sheets to your artwork. Find its label and make a note of the title and date of the artwork and the name of the artist. If you want to be more thorough you can note the dimensions. Then you will be able to compare which work is more original.

Look down the Y column (A-T & i-xxii) and tick the boxes that apply from the X row.

Not all the Y column listings will apply.

The easy and quick method is to use just the "FORMAL CONTENT" and "CONSTRUCTION ELEMENTS" forms. And an even easier method is to just use the Y column entries of these form.

If you add the "BACKGROUND MATERIAL" and "TECHNIQUE" forms you only need to tick which of these are used and also the quality of the work.

From your ticks you will be able to work out a numerical listing for the work e.g.
C 1,3 D 7, F 8.

There is a subjectivity to all entries but this structure begins to make appreciation more objective. Rather than achieve a consensus of understanding create your own understanding of the terms and change them to suit you.

The most subjective entry is the final entry on the X row: quality 1-10. Your view on this will change with the more works you see.

Definitions of each category are given in each chapter. These are loose as it is almost impossible to give precise definitions of terms. Trying to do so would make the system unusable.

The system works for paintings, sculptures, installations and performances. The complexity of video and digital art is not fully addressed though categories have been included to record this work also.

# 2 FORMAL CONTENT

| *a* | X | 1 | 2 | 3 | 4 | 5 | 6 | 7 | 8 | | Quality 1-10 |
|---|---|---|---|---|---|---|---|---|---|---|---|
| Y | **FORMAL CONTENT & STYLE** | S I M P L E | C O M P L E X | O R G A N I S E D | R A N D O M | S Q U A R E | C U R V E | T R U E  F O R M | D I S T O R T I O N | | |
| A | TEXT & SYMBOLS | | | | | | | | | | |
| B | SHAPE | | | | | | | | | | |
| C | PATTERN | | | | | | | | | | |
| D | REPRESENTATION | | | | | | | | | | |
| E | FIGURE | | | | | | | | | | |
| F | 2D | | | | | | | | | | |
| G | 2D ILLUSION 3D | | | | | | | | | | |
| H | a) 3D SCULPT URE | | | | | | | | | | |
| H | b) INSTALLA-TION | | | | | | | | | | |
| H | c) DIORAMA | | | | | | | | | | |
| I | CONCEPT | | | | | | | | | | |

## Y COLUMN (Content)

### A. TEXT & SYMBOLS
The inclusion of letters, words, numbers and symbols. These differ to pictograms e.g. Chinese characters and Egyptian hieroglyphs, which are often abstract forms and shapes, e.g. B and E.

### B. SHAPE
These are basically any kind of shape squares, circles, triangles, cubes, spheres and pyramids etc. It is basically the differentiation between having a form and being formless or amorphous.

### C. PATTERN
Repeated designs, shapes and forms.

### D. REPRESENTATION
Creation of images of beings, objects and places whether imaginary or real, simple or complex.

### E. FIGURE
Specific category of representation for the human figure as it is so prevalent and significant in art.

### F. 2D
A flat picture plane.

### G. 2D ILLUSION 3D
A flat picture plane that is marked to appear like a perspective space or a solid object.

## H. a) 3D SCULPTURE

A physical object that exists in more than 2 dimensions and exhibited free standing from a wall. Exceptions to this definition but are still included are a "frieze" which is a combination of a 2D picture and 3D sculpture and is mounted on a wall, and a "mobile" which is hung from a ceiling or upper support.

Some confusion can arise, e.g. when filling in the X row a difference between a figure (E) that is simple and a sculpture (H) that might be complex can be shown. Or a complex figure (E) is rendered very simply and elegantly as a sculpture (H).

## H. b) INSTALLATION

3D space in which the  viewer moves. This is different to a sculpture because it doesn't need an object in the space.

## H. c) DIORAMA

3D scene in which the viewer doe not move around and may contain a sculpture or model

## I. CONCEPT

This relates to the thoughts and ideas around a piece of work being a significant material element of the work. Almost all works have a degree of conceptual input, but this category is for work where the concept is a deliberate part of the work.
Some contemporary conceptual artwork is deliberately low quality, this can be marked as low quality in one area but high quality in Conceptual.

## *X ROW (Style)*

### 1. SIMPLE
A small number of elements. Your understanding of "simple" will vary as your analysis develops. There is no hard and fast definition just what you feel is simple and complex. It is a matter of comparison.

### 2. COMPLEX
A large number of elements.

### 3. ORGANISED
There is significant order in the composition of the work.

### 4. RANDOM
The work has the appearance of not being created with order and this may be deliberate or without thought. Some artists will deliberately place objects into a configuration that appears random. This would be classed as random with a conceptual element.

### 5. SQUARE
Sharp corners and edges. Can be 2D or 3D.

### 6. CURVE
Rounded corners. Can be 2D or 3D.

### 7. TRUE FORM
Resembles what is being represented.

### 8. DISTORTION
Deliberately does not resemble what is being represented. This is not to be confused with an average young child's drawing which is a low quality True Form.

---

# 3 CONSTRUCTION ELEMENTS

| b | X | 1 | 2 | 3 | 4 | 5 | 6 | 7 | 8 | 9 | |
|---|---|---|---|---|---|---|---|---|---|---|---|
| Y | CONSTR-UCTION ELEMENTS + STYLE | LOOSE/ HAZY / EXPRESSIVE | PRECISE | ORGANISED | RANDOM/ CHAOS | SQUARE | CURVE | THICK | THIN | INTENSITY | Quality 1-10 |
| J | OUTLINE | | | | | | | | | | |
| K | COLOUR FIELD | | | | | | | | | | |
| L | SMUDGE/BLUR | | | | | | | | | | |
| M | DAUBS | | | | | | | | | | |
| N | DOTS | | | | | | | | | | |
| O | LINES | | | | | | | | | | |
| P | DRIPS | | | | | | | | | | |
| Q | 2D SHAPES | | | | | | | | | | |
| R | 3D SHAPE | | | | | | | | | | |
| S | PHOTOGRAPH | | | | | | | | | | |
| T | FOUND OBJECTS | | | | | | | | | | |
| U | LIVING BEINGS | | | | | | | | | | |
| V | COLOUR | | | | | | | | | | |
| W | MONO-CHROME | | | | | | | | | | |
| X | LIGHTNESS | | | | | | | | | | |
| Y | CONTRAST | | | | | | | | | | |
| Z | SATURATION | | | | | | | | | | |

## Y COLUMN (Elements)

### J. OUTLINE
Whether the forms have lines drawn around them or to define them. Lines can have varying forms 1-8.

### K. COLOUR FIELD
An area of colour. This can exist on its own or be inside lines or demarked areas.

### L. SMUDGE/BLUR
Somewhere between a line and a colour field.

### M. DAUBS
Marks made by a pressured application of the paint brush.

### N. DOTS
Lighter application of paint from the end of the brush – crosses over with daubs. Can also be flicked from a brush or blown from a straw etc.

### O. LINES
Short lines that are applied and are not outlines.

### P. DRIPS
The free application of paint by its falling.

### Q. 2D SHAPES
Flat forms that do not have perspective shape.

## R. 3D SHAPE
Forms that have shape in a 3D space. This can refer to the illusion created in a painting or to actual objects. It differs from F, G & H as it is about these shapes being used as elements of construction – like bricks and mosaic tiles. F, G & H.

## S. PHOTOGRAPH
Photograph can be digital or analogue.

## T. FOUND OBJECTS
These objects taken from everyday life can be 2D or 3D and incorporated as collage (2D) or assemblage (3D).

## U. LIVING BEINGS
This can include performance art and living sculpture, e.g. surrealist works. Also inclusion of largely complete dead creatures and skeletons before they are broken into elements (e.g. bones and leather).

V. COLOUR Full spectrum of colour. A separate table for colours and colour theory can be developed. but here is secondary to other formal and construction elements.

W. MONOCHROME Grayscale or tinted shades of a particular colour, e.g. sepia, red or blue tints etc

X. LIGHTNESS the level of light and pastel as opposed to dark and monochrome

Y. CONTRAST the chiaroscuro or contrast between light and dark or between different colours

Z. SATURATION or how intense the colours are

## *X ROW (Style)*

### 1. LOOSE/HAZY /EXPRESSIVE
boundaries are blurred and non-linear and may merge.

### 2. PRECISE
the definition of the item or feature is clear to see and clearly defined.

### 3. ORGANISED
there is significant order in the composition of the the work.

### 4. RANDOM / CHAOS
the work has the appearance of not being created with order and this may be deliberate or without though.

### 5. SQUARE
very sharp corners and bends

### 6. CURVE
rounded edges and corners

### 7. THICK
the application of paint or material is substantial

### 8. THIN
sparse paint or material is used.

### 9. INTENSITY
Particularly for light, contrast and colour XYZ

# 4 BACKGROUND MATERIAL

| c | BACKGROUND MATERIAL | | Quality 1-10 |
|---|---|---|---|
| i | CANVAS | | |
| ii | PAPER | | |
| iii | PENCIL | | |
| iv | INK | | |
| v | OIL | | |
| vi | WATERCOLOUR | | |
| vii | ACRYLIC | | |
| viii | MARBLE | | |
| ix | STONE | | |
| x | METAL | | |
| xi | WOOD | | |
| xii | ORGANIC | | |
| xiii | ENVIRONMENT | | |
| xiv | PHOTO PRINT | | |
| xv | ARTIFICIAL | | |
| xvi | ANALOGUE | | |
| xvii | DIGITAL | | |
| xviii | SOUND | | |

i. CANVAS
cloth based background – primed or unprimed.

ii. PAPER
wood pulp based but can also be rice paper, skin parchment, cardboard etc.

iii. PENCIL
graphite, charcoal and similar coloured mediums

iv. INK
liquid colouring

v. OIL
thick organic colour

vi. WATERCOLOUR
thin water based colour

vii. ACRYLIC
water based and thicker colour

viii. MARBLE
marble, granite and other dense stones.

ix. STONE
Limestone, sandstone, chalk and stones made of granular particles.

x. METAL
iron, bronze, silver, steel, gold etc.

xi. WOOD
tree based wood, not processed into paper.

xii. ORGANIC
plant matter

xiii. ARTIFICIAL
human made materials, e.g. plastics,

xiv. ENVIRONMENT
Not meaning the same as ecology or Environmentalism, rather the space and locality.

xv. PHOTO PRINT
different kinds of printed photographic medium

xvi. ANALGOUE work that exists in non-physical form, on television or video.

xvii. DIGITAL
work that exists in non-physical form on computer or mobile phone.

xviii. SOUND
Noise and music (which can be live or recorded).

# 5 TECHNIQUE

| *d* | TECHNIQUE | | Quality 1-10 |
|---|---|---|---|
| xix | CHISELLED | | |
| xx | MODELLED | | |
| xxi | CAST | | |
| xxii | GLUED/WELDED | | |
| xxiii | CUT | | |
| xxiv | SCREWED/FIXED | | |
| xxv | PAINTED | | |
| xxvi | COLLAGED | | |
| xxvii | PHOTOGRAPHED | | |
| xxviii | SCANNED | | |
| xxix | FILMED | | |
| xxx | PERFORMED | | |
| xxxi | PRINTED | | |
| xxxii | DECONSTRUCTED / DISMANTLED | | |

xix. CHISELLED
material is removed

xx. MODELLED
material is added

xxi. CAST
liquid material poured into a mould and then solidifies.

xxii. GLUED/WELDED
material is fixed to another material with the chemical action of a different material

xxiii. CUT
significant amounts of material is divided (and possibly removed) or marks are incised.

---

xxiv. SCREWED/FIXED
object is fixed with the physical connection of a different object

xxv. PAINTED
surface decoration is applied

xxvi. COLLAGED
pre-made items are added as collage or bricolage

xxvii. PHOTOGRAPHED
still image is instantaneously captured by use of a camera whether analogue or digital

xxviii. SCANNED
still image captured by use of device that records data sequentially following a program, can be 2D or 3D

xxix. FILMED
moving image captured by use of a camera whether analogue or digital

xxx. PERFORMED
work is the actions and processes involved. A product isn't the main outcome – though it can have outcome products.

xxxi. PRINTED
where a liquid is solidified into a particular shape and can be onto a medium e.g. paper or can be free standing e.g. stereo-lithography 3D computer printing.

xxxii. DECONSTRUCTED / DISMANTLED
elements are broken-up and can be re-used in a work.

# 6 CASE STUDIES

Entries for the easiest method of just the Y column entries of Formal Content and Construction Elements form are given in **bold**.

"Bottle of Vieux Marc, Glass, Guitar and Newspaper" 1913, Pablo Picasso **ABDIJQRT**
A1,5.6/B1,4,5,6/D1,8/I2/J2/Q2,4/R4/T2,4/i/ii/xxii/xxv/xxvi
"Weeping Woman" 1937, Pablo Picasso **BEFGIJK**
B2,3,5/E1,3,4,5,8/F2,4,5/G2,3,4,5/I2/J2,7/K2/i/xxv
"Mona Lisa" 1503-6, Leonardo da Vinci **EH**
E2,6,7/H2/viii/xix
"Marilyn" 1967, Andy Warhol **EJK**
E1,7,8/J2/K1,4/i/xvi/xxvii/xxxi
"Angel of the North" 1998, Anthony Gormley **EHT**
E2,6,8/H1,8/T2,5/x/xx/xxi
"The Physical Impossibility of Death in the Mind of Someone Living" 1991, Damien Hirst **HITV**
H1,3,5,6,7/I1/T2/V2,6/xii/xv/xxvi
"One Ball Total Equilibrium Tank" 1985, Jeff Koons **HIT**
H1,3,5,6,7/I1/T2/xv/xxvi
"My Bed" 1998, Tracey Emin **HT**
H1,4,7/T4/xii/xv/xxvi
"Red Room Parents" 1994, Louise Bourgeoise **HT**
H1,4,7/T4/xii/xv/xxvi
"Lipstick (Ascending) on Caterpillar Tracks" 1969, Claus Oldenburg **DHT**
D1,7/H1,7/T3/x,xv,xxii,xxx
Giacometti **EHL**
E1,8/H8/L8/x/xx/xxi
Square Malevich **BIKQ**
B1,5/I2/K2/Q2/i/xxv
"Courier II" Robert Ryman 1985 **BIKQ**
B1,5/I2/K2/Q2/x/xxv

# BIBLIOGRAPHY

"The Art Book" Phaidon

Harping, Patricia "Introduction to Controlled Vocabularies: Terminology for Art, Architecture, and Other Cultural Works", Getty Research Institute. 2013

Hook, Philip "Breakfast at Sotheby's: An A-Z of the Art World" Penguin 2013

Wier, Albert E. "Thesaurus of the Arts" Putnam Sons 1943

Wilson, Simon & Lack, Jessica "The Tate Guide To Modern Art Terms", Tate Publishing 2008

"About the AAT (Art and Architecture Thesaurus)" http://www.getty.edu/pf/PF J. Paul Getty Trust 2010

"Data Standards and Guidelines" http://www.getty.edu/research/conducting research/standards/ J. Paul Getty Trust 2010

"CCO (Cataloging Cultural Objects) Selections" http://vraweb.org/ccoweb/cco/selections.html

# APPENDIX

## Register Of Originality - Rationale

Like many artists, I had worked for years, putting on exhibitions and submitting my work to galleries, only to be rejected. I couldn't understand why galleries weren't interested in my work and they refused to give any reasons.

Then I would see similar work appearing to great acclaim years later. I came to the opinion that the art world needed regulations for how they select art as they were completely unaccountable.

This unaccountability meant that famous artists could plagiarise unknown artists with impunity and also meant that discrimination could occur in the selection of art works.

Below are some of the reasons for a Register of Originality.

### Q & A

Q. But isn't art all subjective. You know "Beauty is in the eye of the beholder" and all that.'

A. There was once a consensus amongst scholars about the principles of classical art. And now, even though modern art is about ideas as well as beauty, it can still be systematised. But the industry doesn't appear to want a system. They want to be free to pick and choose art on a whim, so to counter this and to ensure fairness, regulations are needed.

Q. Surely you can't regulate subjective choices.

A. No, that's a fallacy. They aren't subjective. Classical art has formal "standards" based on originality, draughtsmanship, composition, form, tone, perspective, brush-stroke, colour, light, narrative, meaning, etc. And Modern Art kept many of these standards but now they've all been over-ruled by the whim of rich, white, male collectors.

Q. But wouldn't regulations just destroy creativity?'

A. No, regulation would ensure maximum creativity occurs, because it would stop the same old ideas and styles of work from being repeated and passed off as original and would mean that the creative contribution of all kinds of people would be valued. But racist, sexist, anti-religious art continues to flourish because the art world is controlled by white, middle class bankers and corporations who are against regulations The Register would clearly highlight statistical evidence of any kinds of discrimination. Because there is no regulation of the way that art is chosen all kinds of unconscious discrimination occurs. Curators need to be held responsible for the decisions they make.

Q. Surely the best art has always been commissioned by the rich.

A. That's the problem. The system of the rich selecting art hasn't changed since the times of the Medici family in Renaissance Italy. And the Medicis murdered and cheated their way to the top and even put their own corrupt Pope into power. We should move to a more enlightened ate.

Q. But surely this selection is just artistic preference.

A. No, it's not a preference, it's bias, and is clear in the violent work promoted by individual collectors such as Charles Saatchi, work that mocks religion, works by artists like Damien Hirst. If the work was kept in private collections it would be acceptable but it is promoted through the media as being artistic and that it should be accepted as such by the public.

To protest against an this unfair system and to try and bring in reform, in 2005, I began a case at the Employment Tribunals, claiming that the Trustees and the Director (Sir Nicholas Serota) of the Tate Galleries, were guilty of religious discrimination for only showing a small amount of religious contemporary art and of that only art that was offensive to Christians.

The case was dismissed after two years on a technicality (that my performance art work was over "goods and services" and not "performance of work"). The Judges also thought that discrimination would be difficult to prove. I had proposed the Register of Originality as a way to overcome this difficulty but this was ignored.

Q. Are you sure there is discrimination against artists?'

A. The statistics clearly showed that the works presented at public galleries have bias, e.g. are atheistic, expressed some kind of vague mysticism or were directly offensive towards Christianity. "Religious" art was not included. At best the Tate showed the spirituality of artists like, Jackson Pollock and Mark Rothko. At worst they showed anti-religious works like Gilbert & George's "Shit Christ", Sarah Lucas' "Christ made out of Cigarettes," and Chris Ofilli's "The Holy Virgin Mary" surrounded with pornographic images. And none of these are even particularly original. They are just derived from Andres Serrano "Piss Christ," a 1987 photograph of a crucifix in urine.

Q. As a public gallery don't the acquisitions of the Tate just reflect the interests of the broader art world.

A. And that's the problem. This broader art world is run by oil corporations and financial institutions. These are unregulated, "subjective" choices. This whole agenda is controlled by collectors and curators who are linked to the banks and oil companies. And any regulation, through a Register, will revolutionise the art world – if it becomes popular from the ground up. Top down regulation has been weak.

# FORMAL CONTENT

| *a* | X | 1 | 2 | 3 | 4 | 5 | 6 | 7 | 8 | | Quality 1-10 |
|-----|---|---|---|---|---|---|---|---|---|---|--------------|
| Y | **FORMAL CONTENT & STYLE** | S I M P L E | C O M P L E X | O R G A N I S E D | R A N D O M | S Q U A R E | C U R V E | T R U E F O R M | D I S T O R T I O N | | |
| A | TEXT & SYMBOLS | | | | | | | | | | |
| B | SHAPE | | | | | | | | | | |
| C | PATTERN | | | | | | | | | | |
| D | REPRESENTATION | | | | | | | | | | |
| E | FIGURE | | | | | | | | | | |
| F | 2D | | | | | | | | | | |
| G | 2D ILLUSION 3D | | | | | | | | | | |
| H | a) 3D SCULPTURE | | | | | | | | | | |
| H | b) INSTALLA-TION | | | | | | | | | | |
| H | c) DIORAMA | | | | | | | | | | |
| I | CONCEPT | | | | | | | | | | |

# CONSTRUCTION ELEMENTS

| b | X | 1 | 2 | 3 | 4 | 5 | 6 | 7 | 8 | 9 | |
|---|---|---|---|---|---|---|---|---|---|---|---|
| Y | CONSTR-UCTION ELEMENTS + STYLE | LOOSE/ HAZY / EXPRESSIVE | PRECISE | ORGANISED | RANDOM/ CHAOS | SQUARE | CURVE | THICK | THIN | INTENSITY | Quality 1-10 |
| J | OUTLINE | | | | | | | | | | |
| K | COLOUR FIELD | | | | | | | | | | |
| L | SMUDGE/BLUR | | | | | | | | | | |
| M | DAUBS | | | | | | | | | | |
| N | DOTS | | | | | | | | | | |
| O | LINES | | | | | | | | | | |
| P | DRIPS | | | | | | | | | | |
| Q | 2D SHAPES | | | | | | | | | | |
| R | 3D SHAPE | | | | | | | | | | |
| S | PHOTOGRAPH | | | | | | | | | | |
| T | FOUND OBJECTS | | | | | | | | | | |
| U | LIVING BEINGS | | | | | | | | | | |
| V | COLOUR | | | | | | | | | | |
| W | MONO-CHROME | | | | | | | | | | |
| X | LIGHTNESS | | | | | | | | | | |
| Y | CONTRAST | | | | | | | | | | |
| Z | SATURATION | | | | | | | | | | |

# BACKGROUND MATERIAL

| *c* | BACKGROUND MATERIAL | | Quality 1-10 |
|---|---|---|---|
| i | CANVAS | | |
| ii | PAPER | | |
| iii | PENCIL | | |
| iv | INK | | |
| v | OIL | | |
| vi | WATERCOLOUR | | |
| vii | ACRYLIC | | |
| viii | MARBLE | | |
| ix | STONE | | |
| x | METAL | | |
| xi | WOOD | | |
| xii | ORGANIC | | |
| xiii | ENVIRONMENT | | |
| xiv | PHOTO PRINT | | |
| xv | ARTIFICIAL | | |
| xvi | ANALOGUE | | |
| xvii | DIGITAL | | |
| xviii | SOUND | | |

# TECHNIQUE

| *d* | TECHNIQUE | | Quality 1-10 |
|---|---|---|---|
| xix | CHISELLED | | |
| xx | MODELLED | | |
| xxi | CAST | | |
| xxii | GLUED/WELDED | | |
| xxiii | CUT | | |
| xxiv | SCREWED/FIXED | | |
| xxv | PAINTED | | |
| xxvi | COLLAGED | | |
| xxvii | PHOTOGRAPHED | | |
| xxviii | SCANNED | | |
| xxix | FILMED | | |
| xxx | PERFORMED | | |
| xxxi | PRINTED | | |
| xxxii | DECONSTRUCTED / DISMANTLED | | |

www.ingramcontent.com/pod-product-compliance
Lightning Source LLC
Chambersburg PA
CBHW061232180526
45170CB00003B/1261